THE MYSTERIES

RUDOLF STEINER

The Mysteries

A Poem for Christmas and Easter by W. J. v. Goethe

A lecture held on December 25, 1907, Cologne

SteinerBooks | 2014

SteinerBooks
An imprint of Anthroposophic Press, Inc.
610 Main Street, Great Barrington, MA 01230
SteinerBooks.org

From a stenographic text, not revised by the lecturer.
Published by Marie Steiner 1931.

Translated from the German by Marianne H. Luedeking.

Front cover image: sketch of a monastery by William Turner (1789-1862)

ISBN: 978-1-62148-080-8 (paperback)
ISBN: 978-1-62148-081-5 (e-book)

A LECTURE BY RUDOLF STEINER

Cologne, December 25, 1907

Those of you who were in the Cathedral of Cologne tonight could see there the lighted letters CMB. As is commonly known, according to the tradition of the Christian church, they represent the names of the Three Wise Men, Caspar, Melchior and Balthasar. These three names evoke very special memories for Cologne. An old legend reports that after some time had passed following their deaths, the remains of the Three Kings, who had become bishops, were brought to Cologne. There is also another legend that tells of a Danish king visiting Cologne who brought along three crowns for the Three Holy Kings. When he returned home he had a dream, in which the Three Kings appeared to him and presented him with three goblets. The first goblet contained gold, the second one incense, and the third one myrrh. When the king awoke, the Three Kings had vanished, but the three goblets remained. There stood in front of him, the three gifts he had received in his dream.

This legend encompasses something very profound. It indicates that in the dream the king rose to a certain insight into the spiritual world, which showed him the symbolic meaning of the Three Kings, of these three Wise Men from the Orient, who offered gold, incense and myrrh at the birth of the Christ Jesus. And from this knowledge the king retained permanent gifts, the three human virtues that are indicated symbolically by gold, incense, and myrrh. These three virtues are self-knowledge in the gold; self-piety, which means the piety of the innermost self, also referred to as self-sacrifice, in the incense; and self-perfection and self development, or the consciousness of the eternal in the self, in the myrrh.

How was it possible that the king could receive these three virtues as gifts from another world? He attained this possibility because he tried with his whole soul to penetrate the deep symbol of the Three Kings who offered their gifts to Christ Jesus.

Many different features lie in this Christ legend, which should lead us deeply into the many different interpretations of the Christ principle—what it means and what it is to accomplish in the world. Among the deepest features of the Christ legend are the adoration and offerings of the Three Magi, the Three Kings from the Orient, and not without a deeper understanding may we approach this fundamental symbol of the Christian tradition. Later the idea was developed that the first King was the representative of the Asiatic peoples; the second King, the representative of the European peoples; and the third King, the representative of the African peoples. More and more one wanted to see Christianity as the religion of earthly harmony and the Three Kings and their Homage as a confluence of the various streams and religious directions in the world, flowing towards the one principle, the Christ principle. At the time when this form of the legend was born, those who had penetrated the mystery principles of esoteric Christianity saw in the Christ principle not merely a force that had intervened in the evolution of humanity, but they saw in the entity embodied in Jesus of Nazareth a cosmic world-force, a force that far exceeded human development of the present time. They saw in the Christ principle a force that represents a human ideal in the far distant future, an ideal that we can approach only if we comprehend the world spiritually. They considered the human being primarily as a small being—a small world—a microcosm that was an image of the macrocosm, the large all-encompassing world that contains everything we can perceive, first of all, with our earthly senses, but which also contains everything that the spirit can perceive; it contained what the lowest and also the most clairvoyant spirit could perceive. That is how the world appeared to the esoteric Christians in the first era. Everything that they saw happening in the sky, everything that they saw happening on earth—thunder and lightning, storm and rain, sunshine and the course of the stars, the rising and setting of the sun, and the rising and setting of the moon—all was outer appearance, an external expression of inner spiritual processes. The esoteric Christians consider the cosmic world the way they observe the human body. When they look at the human body, they see it divided into different parts, head, arms, hands, etc. In looking at the human body, they see the movement of the hands, of the eyes, of the facial muscles, but these movements represent for them the expression of the inner soul and spirit experiences. And thus, just as they saw the eternal soul experiences in the movements of the human limbs and parts, so did the esoteric Christians see in the movement of the stars, in the light that streams out to humankind from the stars, in the rising and setting of the sun, in the rising and setting of the moon—in all of that they saw the external expression of divine-spiritual beings that flow through space. For them, all these natural incidents were deeds of the gods, gestures of the gods, mimicry of the divine spiritual beings. The same applied to everything that happened in humanity, when people founded social communities, submitted themselves to ethical commandments and regulated their transactions with each other through laws. It also applied when they created tools from the forces of nature, and indeed with the forces of nature, but in a way which nature did not directly provide. Everything that the human being did more or less unconsciously was, for the esoteric Christians, an external expression of inner divine-spiritual influence. But the esoteric Christians did not limit themselves to such general forms; they indicated very specific gestures, singular parts of the world physiognomy, of the cosmic mimicry, to see in these individual parts specific expressions of the spiritual. When they pointed to the sun, they said, the sun is not only an external physical body; this external physical sun body is the body of a soul-spiritual being, who reigns over those soul-spiritual beings

4

who are the regents, the leaders, of all that happens on earth. These spiritual beings are the guides of all external natural events, but also of everything that happens in the social life and the legal actions among human beings.

When they looked up to the sun, the esoteric Christians revered in the sun the external manifestation of Christ. In the first place, Christ represented for them the soul of the sun, and what the esoteric Christians said was this: From the beginning the sun was the body of the Christ, but the human beings on the earth, and the earth itself, were not yet mature enough to receive the spiritual light of Christ that streams from the sun. Therefore, human beings had to be prepared to receive this Christ light.

Then when the esoteric Christians looked up to the moon, they saw that the moon reflected the light of the sun, but the light was weaker than the direct light from the sun. They told themselves, when I look into the sun with my physical eyes, I am blinded by its shining rays; when I look at the moon, I am not blinded. It gives back the radiant light in a weaker form. In this weakened sunlight that rays down upon the earth from the moon, esoteric Christians recognized the outer expression of the old Jehovah principle, the old law. And they said, before the Christ principle, the sun of justice, could appear on the earth, the old Jehovah principle had to prepare the way, in weakened commandment, by shining this light of justice down onto the earth. Thus, for the esoteric Christians, the spiritual light of the moon, the old Jehovah principle, was the reflected spirit light of the higher Christ principle. And along with followers of the oldest mysteries, the esoteric Christians saw in the sun—even until deep into the Middle Ages—the expression of the spiritual light that ruled the earth, the Christ light; in the moon, they saw the expression of the reflected Christ light, which in its direct form would blind humanity. And in the earth itself the esoteric Christians saw, along with the followers of the oldest mysteries, that which at times covered or hid the blinding sunlight of the spirit. They saw in the earth, as well, the physical expression of a spiritual being, just as they saw in all physical matter the expression of something spiritual. They imagined that when the sun shines perceptibly down upon the earth from spring through summer and elicits all the sprouting and growing life, and when it has reached its zenith in the long days of summer, the esoteric Christians then visualized that the sun brought about all the external sprouting life. In the plants that sprout from the soil, in the animals that at this time could develop their fertility, the esoteric Christians observed the same principle in an external physical manner, which they saw in the spiritual beings, for which the sun is the outer physical expression. Then, however, when the days became shorter as autumn and winter approached, the esoteric Christians said: the sun withdraws its physical power more and more from the earth. To the same degree that the physical power of the sun is withdrawn from the earth, the spiritual force grows strong and flows to the earth, as the days become shortest and the nights longest. This time was later fixed as the Christmas festival. Human beings are unable to see the spiritual force of the sun. The esoteric Christians said people would be able to see it if they had the inner power of spiritual vision. Esoteric Christians were still conscious of the basic conviction and cognition that lived in the mystery students from ancient times until modern times.

In those nights, which today are established as the Christmas festival, the mystery students were prepared for perception of inner spiritual vision, so that they could see spiritually what most withdraws its physical powers from the earth during those winter days. In the long, wintery Christmas night the mystery students had reached the point that a vision could appear to them at midnight. The earth was then no longer a sheath for the sun, which stood behind the earth. The earth became transparent for them. They could see the spiritual light of the sun, the Christ light, through the transparent earth. This deep experience for the mystery student is remembered in the expression, "Seeing the sun at midnight."

There are areas where the churches, which are normally open all day, are closed at midday. This is a fact that brings Christianity into connection with the tradition of ancient religions. Within ancient religious confessions the mystery students declared out of their own experiences: At midday when the sun stands highest in the sky, when it displays the strongest physical power, the gods sleep. Thus, they sleep the deepest sleep in the summer, when the sun displays its strongest physical force. But they are most awake during the Christmas night, when the outer physical power of the sun is the weakest.

We observe that all beings that want to develop their outer physical force look up to the sun when the sun ascends in the spring; they strive to receive the outer, physical sun power. However, in the summer, when the sun sends its strongest physical power down to earth, its spiritual force is weakest. But in the winter-midnight, when the sun beams down its weakest physical power, human beings see the spirit of the sun through the earth, which has become transparent for them. The esoteric Christians sensed that by delving deeply into Christian esotericism they could more and more approach the power of inner vision through which they could completely fulfill their feeling, thinking and will impulses by looking into this spiritual sun. Then the mystery student would be led to a vision that had a most important meaning: as long as the earth is opaque, the individual parts are inhabited by human beings who unfold individual religious beliefs, but the unifying bond is wanting. The races of humans are dispersed like the climates and their opinions are diverse on earth, but a uniting bond is not there. To the degree, however, in which human beings begin to penetrate the earth with their gaze to see the sun, to the degree in which the star appears to them through the earth, to that degree the various confessions of humankind join together in a large united brotherhood of humanity. And those individuals who led the big separate masses of humanity in the truth of the higher planes to initiation into the higher worlds were presented as the Wise Men: There were three of them, because at the most diverse places on earth the most diverse forces manifested themselves. Therefore, humankind had to be led in diverse ways. The star that rises behind the earth, however, appears as a uniting force. It guides the dispersed people toward each other, and there they sacrifice to the physical incarnation of the sun-star that had appeared as the star of peace. Thus in a cosmic and human way the religion of peace, harmony, and human brotherhood is brought into connection with the ancient Wise Men, who laid down at the cradle of the incarnated Son of Man the best gifts that they had for humankind.

The legend has held on to this beautifully, in that it said that the Danish king had achieved the knowledge of the Wise Men, the Three Kings. And since he had risen to that level, they left him their three gifts: first, the gift of wisdom in self-knowledge; second, the gift of devoted piety in self-sacrifice; and third, the gift of the victory of life over death in the power and care of the eternal in the self.

All those who have understood Christianity in this manner have seen the deep spiritual-scientific idea of the unification of the religions. They held the firm conviction that whoever embraces Christianity in this fashion can change and achieve the highest level of human development.

One of the last Germans who recognized Christianity in this manner was Goethe, and Goethe has bestowed upon us this type of Christianity, this type of religious compensation, this kind of theosophy, in the profound poem "The Mysteries," which remains incomplete but which shows us in deep, significant ways the inner soul development of a person who is imbued with and convinced of the above mentioned feelings and ideas. First we hear how Goethe wants to point out the pilgrim path of such a person; and he indicates how such a pilgrim path can lead to many erroneous roads, and that it is not easy to find the right one. The pilgrim will need patience and devotion to reach the goal. Those who possess these qualities can find the light they seek. Let's hear the beginning of the poem:

A wondrous song has been for you prepared
Be glad to hear it and call all to our side!
O'er mount and valley leads the path as varied:
Here is the view enclosed, there it is wide.
And when the path leads into thickets there,
Don't think that it may error hide.
At last, when we enough have climbed,
We shall approach our goal in proper time.
But do not think that even being clever
You could resolve the meaning of the song forever.
For many there is much here to be gained
Our Mother Earth produces many blooms.
The one escapes with looks of utter gloom.
The other stays with glad and joyful mood.
Each one his own delight shall know;
For every wanderer shall the wellspring flow.

We are placed into this situation: a pilgrim is introduced to us, who, if we could ask him, could not tell us according to his own understanding what we have just indicated as the esoteric Christian idea, but a pilgrim in whose heart and soul these ideas are alive, transformed into feelings. Not everything is easily found that has been secreted into this poem, which is called "The Mysteries." Goethe indicated it clearly: a process occurs in the life of a human being in whom the highest ideas, thoughts, and imaginations transform themselves into feelings and sensibilities. How does this transformation occur?

We live through many incarnations; from one incarnation to the next. In each one we learn many varied things; each one provides many opportunities to collect new experiences. It is not possible that we carry over each and every detail from one incarnation to the next. When a man is born again, not everything has to revive with him in all the details that he had previously learned. If he has learned a lot during one incarnation, when he then dies and is born again not all of his ideas have to revive with him, but he lives with the fruits of his previous life, with the fruits of his learning. His feelings, his sentiments, are the result of his previous incarnations.

Here, in Goethe's poem, we have a wonderful phenomenon. We encounter a person who, in the simplest childlike words, not spoken out of his intellect and formed ideas, imparts to us the highest wisdom, the fruits, of his previous cognitions. He has transformed these cognitions into feelings and sentiments, and has, therefore, been called to lead others who may even have learned more conceptually. Such a pilgrim with a mature soul who has transformed into immediate feeling and sentiment much of what he had collected as knowledge in prior incarnations...such a pilgrim do we have before us in the person of Brother Marcus. As a member of a secret Brotherhood he is sent out with an important mission to another secret Brotherhood. Through varied landscapes he wanders, and having tired he arrives at a mountain. At last he climbs up the path.... (every detail in this poem has a deep meaning).... Having climbed the mountain, he finds himself in front of a monastery. This monastery is the expression for another Brotherhood to which he has been sent. Above the gate he sees something special. He sees the Cross, but in a particular way: the Cross encircled by roses! Around the Cross, he sees a shining triangle from which rays beam out like from the sun. He now utters a meaningful phrase that can be understood only by someone who knows how often this code is spoken within the secret Brotherhoods: "Who joined the roses to the Cross?" He does not need to interpret the meaning of this deep symbol; it lives in feeling and sentiment within his soul, his mature soul. His mature soul knows everything that this symbol represents. What is the meaning of the Cross? He knows that the Cross expresses manifold things, among them the threefold lower nature of humans, the physical body, ether body, and the astral body. Into this is born the "I," the ego.

Why roses for the "I?" The esoteric Christians joined the roses to the Cross because it contained in the Christ principle the summons to elevate the "I," as it is born into the three bodies, to elevate it to an ever higher and higher "I." Within the Christ principle they saw the power to elevate this "I" to ever higher levels. The Cross is the sign of death with a very distinct meaning. Goethe expresses this beautifully at another place in his writings:

> And so long as you don't possess
> This to die and birth
> You are but a gloomy guest
> On our somber earth.
>
> *The West-East Divan,* "Book of the Singer" (Moganni Nameh)

Die and be born—overcome what has been given to you originally in your three lower bodies. Kill it off, but don't kill it to wish death, but to purify what exists in the three bodies, so that you can conquer in the "I" the power to reach more and more perfection. By killing off what has been given in the three lower bodies, the "I" gains the power of perfecting. In the "I" the Christ shall, within the Christ principle, take up the power of perfecting, even into the blood. Even into the blood shall the power be effective.

The blood is the expression of the "I." The esoteric Christians recognized in the red roses that which in the blood, purified and clarified by the Christ principle, i.e., the purified "I," will guide the human being to his higher being—that which transforms the astral body into the Spirit Self, the ether body into the Life Spirit, and the physical body into Spirit Man. Thus we encounter in the triangle-surrounded Rose-Cross the Christ principle on the Cross, in deep symbolism. Brother Marcus arrives here and realizes that he is at a place where the deepest meaning of Christianity is understood.

> Exhausted from the day's long walk
> Which on high order he did undertake,
> Leant on his staff, like pious pilgrims' do,
> Thus Brother Marcus, leaving road and path,
> Requiring modest drink and fare
> Arrived at Evening Bells within the valley
> In hopes of finding in this wooded dale
> A hospitable shelter for the night.

> Along the mountain now before him
> He spies the traces of a little path.
> He walks along the path, which curves
> And winds itself around the mountain rocks
> And soon he sees himself above the vale,
> The sun's bright rays are shining here again
> And with relief and inner joy
> He sees the mountain top quite near.

> And next to it the setting sun
> Still splendid between darkened clouds.

Collecting forces now to mount the crest
He hopes his efforts will be blessed.
Murmuring to himself he says
"Now we shall see
If any humans live in this vicinity."
He climbs and listens and is like re-born:
His ears just heard a church bell's pretty sound.

Now having climbed at last the mountain top
He sees a gentle wavy dale,
His quiet eye with pleasure shines:
Before the woods he sees at last
A well proportioned building on the grass,
Illumined by the sun's last rays.
He hastens through the meadow, damp with dew
Towards the cloister which invites his view.

Arriving at the calm and quiet place
Which fills his mind with hope and peace
He sees upon the arch of the closed gate
A most mysterious image fastened there .
He stands and muses; lowly murmurs
Words of devotion spilling from his heart.
He stands and thinks: "What does it mean?"
The sun has set; the bells no longer toll.

The sign he sees so mightily installed
That serves to all the world as comfort and as hope
To which have bound them many thousand souls
To which so many thousand hearts implore

Which overcame the bitter force of death
Which flutters on so many victory flags:
New strength fills now his tired limbs.
He sees the cross and down he casts his eyes.
He feels anew the source of all salvation,
The faith he feels of more than half a world.
But new and forceful meanings pierce his heart
As this new sign his eyes behold:
The cross with roses tightly wound.
"Who joined the roses to the cross?"
Tightly are wound the roses on the cross
To soften the stark hardness of the wood.

And little silver clouds are floating
To elevate the roses and the cross.
From out the center shines a sacred life
Of threefold rays from out a single point:
No words surround the sacred sign
That would reveal the myst'ry's sense and clarity.
Dusk does descend now more and more.
He stands and thinks and feels himself restored.

The spirit of profound Christianity which can be found in this building is expressed by this Cross wound about with roses; and as the pilgrim now enters into the building, he is truly received by this spirit. As he enters, he becomes aware that in this house there reigns not this or that religion of the world, but that here reigns the higher unity of all religions of the world. Within the building he informs one of the old members of the

Brotherhood why he has come and on whose orders. He is received and hears that in this house, completely withdrawn, lives a Brotherhood of twelve men. These Twelve Brothers are representatives of varied groups of peoples on the earth; each one of the Brothers is a representative of a religious belief. You won't find that someone would be accepted into the Brotherhood when still young in years, still immature. To become accept-able, one has to have looked around in the world; one has to have overcome the worlds' joys and sorrows; one has to have worked and arrived at a free view over one's closely limited field. Only then can one be accepted into the circle of Twelve. And these Twelve — each one rep-resents a different religious belief of the world — live in peace and harmony with each other because they are guided by a Thirteenth, who ranks way above the oth-ers in perfection of the human self, who surpasses all in the wide array of human circumstances. And how does Goethe indicate that this One is the representative of the true esotericism? It is indicated by Goethe that he is the bearer of the Creed of the Rosy Cross. The Brothers confide, "he was among us; but now we are in deep mourning because he wants to leave us. He wants to depart from us. He finds it appropriate to depart from us; he wants to rise into higher regions, where he no longer needs to appear in a physical body."

He may rise, because he has developed to the point, which Goethe explains thus: "in every confession exists the possibility to approach the highest purity." When each one of the twelve religions matures to bring harmony, then the Thirteenth, who had previously established this harmony externally, can vanish. In a fine way it is explained how one can gain this perfection of the self. First we are told the life history of the Thirteenth; but the Brother who welcomed our Brother Marcus knows a lot more about the Thirteenth, which the leader of the Twelve himself may not tell. Some traits of profound esoteric meaning are being told to Brother Marcus by one of the Twelve. It's being told of the Thirteenth that when he was born a star predicted his life on earth. This is an immediate connection to the Star that led the Three Holy Kings, and to its meaning. This star has a permanent meaning. It designates the path to self-knowledge, self-sacrifice, and self-perfection. It is the star that opens understanding for the gifts that the Danish king received through the apparition in his dream, the star that appears at the birth of those who are mature enough to receive the Christ principle into themselves. But there is more. It is shown that he had developed himself to the height of religious harmony that brings the harmony and peace of the soul. It is deeply symbolized by the tale that when the Thirteenth appeared in the world a hawk descended, but instead of causing havoc, it spread harmony among the doves. More still do we learn. When his little sister lay in the cradle, an adder wound itself around her. The Thirteenth, himself still a child, killed the snake. A wonderful indication of how a mature soul in earliest youth can kill the adder, i.e., overcome the lower astral being—because only a mature soul after many incarnations can achieve something like that. The adder (snake) is the expression for the lower astral being; the sister is his own ether body, surrounded by the astral body. He killed the adder for his sister. Furthermore, we are told how obediently he does everything that the parents demand. He obeys the rough father. The soul transforms its knowledge into ideas and thoughts. Thus the soul develops healing forces, whereby healing in the world can be effected. Magic powers are developed, which are expressed in the tale when he causes, with his sword, a well to spring forth from a rock. One finds here how his soul follows the track of the Bible. Thus, by and by, the Master matures. He is the representative of humankind, the Chosen One, who as the Thirteenth here in the community of the Twelve, in the large secret order under the symbol of the Rose-Cross, has shouldered for humanity the mission to harmonize the varying confessions in the world. Thus we are at first made aware, in a profound manner, of the soul condition of the one who has led the Brotherhood of the Twelve.

At last he knocks, high stand the stars within the sky
And brightly shine upon him now.
The gate is opened, and he is received with joy,
With open arms, with ready hands.
He tells from whence he comes, from which far
    distant place
The higher beings' orders had him sent.
Amazed they listen; a stranger had they honored him;
Now do they honor the most welcome guest.

Each one crowds near to listen well
And feels himself be moved by secret force
They hold their breath not to disturb the guest
Since every word resounds within their chest.
What he relates acts like profoundest rules
Of wisdom, which from children's lips resound:
In openness, in innocence of geste
He seems a man from yet a different plane.
"Be welcome, welcome!" one old man calls out,
"If hope and consolation come with you;
"You look at us and see we are oppressed.
"Although the sight of you does move our souls.
"The best of fortunes will be lost to us.
"And fear and worry have us overcome.
"A most important hour brings you here
"To join with us in our time of woe.

"Because the man, who binds us all together
"Whom we call Father, Friend, and Guide
"Who lit the light and valor in our lives
"Will in brief time depart from us.
"He has made known to us that he will soon
"Remove himself from us. Not time or manner
"Of his leaving will he tell. Thus his withdrawal
"Full of secrecy is causing us such bitter, bitter suff'ring.

"You see that all of us are old and grey,
"As nature has assigned us to tranquility.
"We don't accept one young in years,
"Whose heart leads him to leave the world too soon.

"As our lives had known both lust and joys and pain
"The winds no longer buoyed our sails;
"We were allowed with honor here to land,
"With confidence that we a safe port found.
"The noble man who led us to this place
"God's peace rests in his heart.
"Accompanying him on life's long paths
"I well remember olden times' content.
"The hours that in solitude he spends
"Preparing him for our approaching loss.
"What is a man? Why must he leave his life
"With no compense? Why can't he give it for another one?

"That is my only wish; why must I yield it?
"How many have before me gone!
"I mourn so bitterly but him.
"How friendly he would else have greeted thee!
"But he already has transferred this house
"To our own care; but has not chosen yet
"Who should succeed him as our guide
"Though he already lives in mind and spirit far from us.

"Each day he comes for just a fleeting hour
"Talks of his life and more than usual is moved.
"From his own mouth we hear, how providence
"Has led him wondrously in life.
"With care we listen; that not the smallest detail
"Will e'er be lost to our posterity.
"We also write it down, so that the facts
"Remain in memory unaltered, clean and true.

"I would have rather told some tales myself,
"That now I must just listen silently.
"The smallest detail I would not omit;
"Each incident I vividly recall.
"I listen and confess that many times
"I'm not content with his related tale.
"When once I shall retell these things,
"They shall resound more splendidly indeed.

"As a third man I could relate more freely and much more
"How early on a ghostly messenger announced his birth
"To his own mother; that at the celebration of his christening
"A star shone brighter than the rest within the
            evening sky.
"And that with wings widespread a hawk
"Sat down among the doves upon the court
"Not fiercely striking as would be his way
"But peaceably to unity appeared to sway.

"He also modestly concealed that as a child
"He overcame the adder that he found
"Around his little sister's arm had wound
"And tightened round the sleeping child.
"The nurse had fled and left the baby there.
"The worm he strangled with his own sure hand,
"The mother came and with relief and joy
"Saw her son's feat and thus her daughter's life.

"Again he did omit to talk about the spring
"Of purest water that his sword drew forth,

"From dryest rock; strong like a brook
"It flowed in waves from mountain into dale.
"Silvery clear it still flows strong today
"Just like it first sprang forth out of the rock.
"Witnessing the miracle, his friends
"Did hardly dare to quench their urgent thirst.

"When birth and nature elevate a man
"It is no wonder that in much he shows success:
"One has to praise in him creator's deeds
"Which have weak clay to such high honor raised.
"But when a man through all life's strongest trials
"Prevails upon the worst: conquers himself,
"Then you can point him out with joy and pride
"To others and exclaim: there is a man; he is his
        own.

"All forces urge to forward press, expand,
"To live, to work, now here, now there;
"But opposition hems us in from every side;
"The world's wild stream tows us along with it.
"Within this inner storm and outer strife
"The spirit hears a word that's hard to understand:
"'From the strong force confining all humankind
"'He frees himself who conquers his own self.'"

Such is the man who, conquering himself by van-
quishing the "I" he had been dealt, had become the
leader of the characterized chosen Brotherhood. And
thus he led the Twelve. He has guided them up to the

point that they are now mature enough that he may leave them. Our Brother Markus is now being led further into the rooms where the Twelve are active. How are they active? This activity is of a particularly special kind, and we are being made aware that this activity occurs in the spiritual world. The person whose eyes are directed only to the physical plane, whose senses perceive only the physical and only what is being accomplished in the physical world, cannot easily think that there exists another work and activity that, under certain circumstances, might be more important than what is being accomplished on the physical plane. The work on these higher planes is much more important for humankind. However, the condition must be fulfilled that whoever wants to work on those higher planes must first have absolved his tasks in the physical world. These Twelve had accomplished that. Therefore, their cooperation represented something very exalted in the service for humankind.

Our Brother Markus is introduced into the hall where the Twelve get together for their common meetings, and there he is met in profound symbolism by the manner in which they cooperate. A special symbol, characterizing what each of the Brothers contributes out of his own singular peculiarity, is affixed above his seat. Manifold symbols are there, that in a different significant manner express what each one contributes to the common activity that is effective in the spiritual world, so that these streams flow together here into one stream of spiritual life that flows out into the world and empowers the rest of humanity. These Brotherhoods exist, these centers exist, from which flow out such streams and weave their effect on the rest of humankind.

Brother Markus sees affixed above the seat of the Thirteenth, once again, the Sign of the Cross wound about with roses. This Sign is simultaneously the symbol for the four-part human nature; and the red roses symbolize the purified blood, or "I"-principle, the principle for the higher human. And then he perceives that the special symbols of what this special Sign is meant to overcome are affixed on the right and the left side of the seat of the Thirteenth. On the right he sees the fire-colored dragon that signifies the astral entity of the human being. It was well known within Christian esotericism that the human soul may be dedicated to the three lower bodies. If the soul is thus dedicated, then in it functions the lower life of the threefold embodiment, and that is expressed in the astral perception of the dragon. That is not just a symbol, but a very real representation. The dragon stands for that which must first be overcome. In the passions, in these forces of the astral fire that belong to the physical human being, in this dragon, Christian esotericism — the basis on which this poem has been written and which had spread throughout Europe — saw what had been received by humanity from the hot zone, from the South. From the South originates that part of the human being that humanity has brought along as hot passion, which is directed more to the lower sensuality. As a first impulse

25

to fight and overcome this, one felt the presentiment of the influences that flowed down from the cooler North. The influence of the cooler North, the descending of the "I" into the threefold embodiment of the human being, is expressed in an ancient symbol taken from the starry constellation of the Bear, in extending a hand into the open jaws of a bear. The overcoming of the lower nature of the human being is expressed in the fiery dragon. What has been preserved in the higher nature of the animal is represented by the bear; and the "I" that has developed itself out of the dragon nature is represented in a profound reference by the extending of the hand into the open jaw of the bear. On both sides of the rose-entwined Cross appeared what had to be conquered by the Rose-Cross, and it is the Rose-Cross that encourages humanity to purify itself to ever higher states.

Thus, the poem really shows us the principle of Christianity in the deepest sense and leads us above all to a vision of what should most specially appear before the soul at a festival like the present one.

The eldest of the here remaining Brothers who belong to the Brotherhood expressly explains to Brother Marcus that what they do here together is activity in the spiritual sphere; this is spiritual life. This work for humanity on the spiritual level means something special. The Brothers have experienced life's joys and sorrows; they have fought their battles outside; they have done their work in the outside world. Now they are here, but their work here is by no means accomplished.

On and on goes the work on the further development of humankind. It is now indicated to Brother Marcus: you have now seen as much as is shown a disciple to whom the first gate has been opened. We have shown you the important symbols of how humanity's ascent should be. But the second gate encloses higher mysteries, how work proceeds on humanity from out of the higher worlds. But those mysteries will be opened to you only after longer preparation. Only then may you enter through the other gate. Profound mysteries are expressed in this poem.

"How early was it, that his heart him taught
"That what in him I hardly dare call virtue;
"That he his father's stern command obeyed
"And willingly, however sharp and rough
"The freedom of his youth with service was
        curtailed,
"To which the son with gladness did submit
"As might an orphaned straying boy would do
"Out of necessity, for a small gift.

"Accompanying fighters in the field
"At first on foot, in storm and sunny skies,
"Tend to the horses and the tables set,
"And do the bidding of each warrior old
"Glad and with speed all times he ran
"As messenger, through woods by night and day.
"And thus accustomed just for others in his life
"Hard tasks seemed just to give him joy.

"As during battle he with keen and merry mood
"Picked up the arrows from the ground
"So did he rush to gather healing herbs
"With which to bandage fighters' wounds:
"What he but touched, it quickly healed
"The ill delighted in his hand.
"Who would not look at him with joy?
"Only his father seemed to note him not.

"Light, as a sailing ship without a load
"That lightly sails from port to port
"He bore parental teaching's load
"Obedience was their first and ending word.
"As gladness of the boy, and honor of the youth
"Thus other's than his own will drew him on.
'The father sought in vain new tasks;
"Expecting to demand he had to praise.

"At last the old man, too, had to admit
"And actively promote the son's great worth.
"The roughness of the father disappears
"He gives his son the present of a precious horse
"From all the minor tasks the youth was now
        relieved.
"The dagger was replaced now by a sword
"Thus tested did he join an order
"To which his birth entitled him.

"For days long could report I more to you
"What every listener would set in awe

"His life's account will likened to the tales
"Of glorious fame by his descendents be:
"What unbelievable in fables, poetry and tales
"Appears, yet pleases to the mind and heart —
"Perceive it here and do enjoy it more
"Since all is based on true reality.
"And when you ask me for the name
"Of him whom providence did choose
"Whom I have often praised but not enough
"Who unbelievable adventures lived:
"Humanus is his name, the saint, the sage
"The best man whom my eyes have seen
"As to his lineage as the princes call it,
"Together with his ancestors you'll know."

The old man spoke and leave had talked some more
He was so full of all the wondrous things
Which entertain us still in weeks to come
As he will tell them to our eager ears.
But now his tales were broken off
Just as his guest's heart listened full.
The other brothers came and went
And took the word away from him.

The meal has ended. Marcus having thanked
The Lord and, too, his hosts,
Requests a bowl of water plain,
And also that was given him.
He now was led to the great hall
Wherein a curious aspect he perceived.

What he saw there shall not be kept from you
I shall describe it to you conscientiously.
No decoration in it to deceive the eye
A high vault rose above the room
And thirteen chairs stood 'round about the walls
Well ordered like devout a choir
Gracefully carved by skillful hands
A little desk in front of each of them.
One felt to prayer and solemnity devoted here
To restful life and yet communal life.

And thirteen coats of arms he sees displayed.
Above each chair is one arrayed,
But not devoted to ancestral pride.
Yet each appeared importantly adorned
And Brother Marcus burned with eagerness
To learn what each adornment hid.
Upon the center one he sees the sign
A second time: the cross with roses wound about.

The soul can here imagine much
Each object draws attention to itself
Helmets hang over various shields,
And swords and lances here and there
The weapons which you might collect
From battlefields, adorn this place
Here flags and guns from foreign lands
And — do I see it right — there chains and even shackles.

Each brother kneels before his chair
In silent prayer concentrated now;

Short hymns sound from their lips
In which devotion's joy is thus expressed.
The blessing spoken by the faithful brothers
Now to brief sleep that's free from phantasy.
Marcus remains with some, while others go,
And stands observing still.

Though tired yet he wants to wake
For many pictures stir his mind with force.
He sees a fire-colored dragon here
Quenching his thirst in savage flames.
And there an arm within a wild bear's throat
From which a stream of blood is gushing forth.
These two shields equidistant hang
On either side of that which bears the rosy cross.

"You came hither to us on wondrous paths"
The old one friendly speaks again.
"May these symbolic pictures make you stay
"A while, until you learn each hero's deeds
"What's hidden here cannot deciphered be
"Unless in confidence it's shown to thee.
"You may surmise how much was suffered then,
"Was lived, was lost, and what was overcome."

Don't think that only of old times the old man speaks;
He tells: "Much more is happening right here;
"What you do see has meaning more and more
"Some may be covered by a carpet, some by flowers.
"If you so will, prepare yourself.

"You entered, friend, but through the first of doors;
"You have been welcomed in the entrance hall
"But you seem worthy for admittance to the core."

After a brief rest, our Brother Marcus learns at least to have a presentiment of this core. The important symbols of the rise of the human selfhood have left their mark on his soul, and when he is awakened from his short sleep by a signal, he notices a small window, a type of barred opening, and hears a strange triad: three beats on a gong permeated by the sounds of a flute. He cannot see what is happening in the room beyond. We need not be told any more than these few words to indicate in a profound way what awaits human beings when they approach the spiritual world—when they have, through their work on their selfhood, cleansed and perfected themselves so far that they have passed through the astral world and approached the spiritual worlds—those worlds in which are found the prototypes of the things on earth.

When they approach what, in esoteric Christianity, is called heaven, this then appears to them through a world of flowing colors; they enter a world of sounds, the Harmony of the World, the Music of the Spheres. The spiritual world is a world of tones. Those who have developed their "I" toward the higher worlds, will experience these higher worlds. It is Goethe who has brought to clear expression this experience of a world of spiritual sounds in his *Faust*, when he removes Faust into heaven, where the heavenly world is manifest to him through tones.

"The sun resounds in ancient ways
   with brother spheres' competing songs."

The physical sun does not sound, but the spiritual sun does. Goethe maintains that image when he sets Faust, after long wanderings, up into the spiritual world. (*Faust*, second part): "Sounding loud for spirit ears / is the new day given birth." "It drums, it trumpets. The unheard will not be heard."

Through the symbolic world of the astral, human beings, when they have developed themselves further upward, approach the world of the Music of the Spheres. Softly, softly, going outside, after passing though the first gate (the gate of the astral), our Brother Marcus perceives the sound of the inner world, which lies behind our outer world. It is this world that alters the lower world of the astral into the higher world, which is permeated by the triad. And as we enter into the higher world, the human lower nature changes into the higher threefold unity; our astral body becomes the Spirit Self; our ether body, the Spirit Life, and the physical body becomes the Spirit Man. He senses at first in the Music of the Spheres the triad of the higher nature, and as he becomes one with this Music of the Spheres, he senses for the first time something of the rejuvenation of the human being who enters into a connection with spiritual worlds. Like in a dream he sees the rejuvenated humanity in the form of three youths gliding through the garden. That is the moment when the soul of Marcus awakes in the morning out of the darkness, but where the darkness still remains somewhat; the soul has not yet overcome it completely. But exactly at this moment the soul is able to look little by little into the spiritual world. It can look into the spiritual world and—when the summer noon has passed, when the sun becomes ever weaker and the winter has arrived, when at midnight there shines through the earth— can see the Christ principle in the Holy Night. Owing to the Christ principle, the human being is lifted up to the higher threefold unity, which presents itself to Brother Marcus in the three youths who represent the rejuvenated human soul. That is what Goethe has expressed in the verse:

> "…And so long as you don't possess
> This To Die and Birth
> You are but a gloomy guest
> On our somber earth."

Every year anew, to the one who understands esoteric Christianity, the Holy Night shall point out that whatever happens in the outer world is but mimicry, gesture, for the interior spiritual occurrence. The external power of the sun expends itself in the spring and the summer sun. In the Holy Scriptures this external sun force, which is only the announcement of the inner spiritual force of the sun, is expressed in St. John; while the actual inner spiritual force is expressed in the Christ. And while the physical power of the sun wanes more and more, the spiritual power rises and becomes stronger and stronger, until it is strongest during Christmastime. This is the basis for the words in the Gospel of St. John: "I must sink; but He must rise." (Free rendering) And he rises and rises, and appears there where the sun force has again reached its outer physical power. In order for human beings to be able now to revere and adore in this outer physical force, this interior spiritual sun force, they must recognize the meaning of the Christmas festival. For those who do not recognize this important meaning, this new power of the sun remains nothing more than the old physical sun. However, those who have familiarized themselves with the impulses that esoteric Christianity and the Christmas festival should provide them will see, in the growing power of the sun body, the outer body of the inner Christ that shines through the earth, which He enlivens and fructifies, so that the earth itself becomes the bearer of the Christ power, of the Spirit of the earth. Thus, what is born for us in the Christmas night is being reborn anew each time. The Christ Being permits us to perceive the microcosm within the macrocosm, and this perception will guide us higher and ever higher.

What for humanity has already for a long time become something external — the Festivals — will reappear for us in their profoundest meaning, when we are lead by this deep esotericism to the knowledge that whatever happens in outer nature, like thunder and lightning, sunrise and sunset, moonrise and setting, is gesture and physiognomy of spiritual existence. And at the important points that are indicated by our Festivals

we ought to recognize that also within the spiritual
world important events take place. Then will we be
guided toward the rejuvenating spiritual power that is
indicated by the three youths, which the "I" can win
only by devotion to the exterior world, not by egois-
tically closing itself off from it. But there is no devotion to the exterior world, if this exterior world is not
permeated by the Spirit. That this Spirit shall reappear
each year anew for all humanity, even for the weakest, as a "Light that shines in the darkness," should
each year be inscribed anew into the hearts and souls
of human beings.

That is what Goethe wanted to express in this poem,
"The Mysteries." It is a poem for Christmas, and for
Easter as well. It wants to clarify deep mysteries of esoteric Christianity. When we let it affect us—what he
wanted to indicate of the deep mysteries of Rosicrucian
Christianity—when we even absorb even only a part of
this force, we shall become missionaries for at least a
few in our surroundings; we shall celebrate the Festivals
in a spiritual way, and full of life.

A dull dark bell tone awakens our friend
From a brief sleep within a quiet cell.
This son of heaven hurries and with happy speed
Follows the call to early prayer.
He dresses quickly, rushes to the door,
His heart runs to the chapel eagerly,
Obedient, quiet, winged by prayer
He tries the latch and finds the door is locked.

And as he listens hears the hollow sound
Anew of three strong beats of brass on brass;
Not stroke of clock, and not the chime of bells,
The tone of flute is joined from time to time
To the strange resonance, that to define is hard,
It moves the heart to joyful mood,
Inviting gravely, like with songs
Contented pairs meandering about.

He hurries to the window, hopes to see
What's both confusing and elating him.
He sees the day arising in the East
The sky festooned with lighted stripes
And – should he really trust his eyes –
A curious light is gliding through the yard:
Three youths with lanterns in their hands
Are quickly wending through the paths.
He clearly sees the gleam of their white robes
Fitting and suiting well their shape;
Their curly hair with flowered wreaths
And roses girdling 'round their waist.
It seems as though they came from nightly dances
From joyful toil refreshed and fair.
They hurry now and like the stars
Extinguishing their lanterns vanish in the far.

www.ingramcontent.com/pod-product-compliance
Lightning Source LLC
Chambersburg PA
CBHW021148020426
42331CB00005B/951